30 Days

To Stop Giving A

Shit

A Mindfulness Program with a Touch of Humor

Corin Devaso

Copyright © JV 2021

Share your journey!

Let people know you're practicing mindfulness! Post a picture of the cover and include #30DaysNow via social media. Our various guides share the same lessons, so you can see how others are using mindfulness on their journey!

Don't forget that each exercise has a unique hashtag for online sharing.

This book is meant to be a guide only, and does not guarantee specific results. If the lessons and exercises in this book are followed, change can occur for certain people. Results vary from person to person; some people may not need to complete the thirty days to experience change, but it's encouraged that the entire program be read completely through at least once.

The last half of the book consists of blank note pages that the reader can use in conjunction with the exercises for each day. The reader is encouraged to utilize the note pages; though it's not necessary.

Give the gift of mindfulness. See similar guides at www.30DaysNow.com if you wish to purchase a book for a loved one. **See the disclosure below.**

Disclosure (Shared Lessons and Exercises):

Keep in mind that our mindfulness guides share the same lessons and exercises, so there is no need to purchase more than one book; unless you are sharing with a group or giving the guides as gifts. Our mindfulness guides are created for various topics; however, they utilize the same lessons and exercises, so please be aware of this before purchasing. For example, *30 Days to Stop Giving a Shit* will mostly have the same lessons and exercises as *30 Days to Reduce Anxiety* and so forth. By reading just one of our guides, you'll be able to apply the same lessons and exercises to multiple areas of your life.

Enjoy your journey of self-discovery!

Contents

Preface..4

Day 1..7
Day 2..8
Day 3..9
Day 4..10
Day 5..11
Day 6..12
Day 7..13
Day 8..14
Day 9..15
Day 10..16
Day 11..17
Day 12..18
Day 13..19
Day 14..20
Day 15..21
Day 16..22
Day 17..23
Day 18..24
Day 19..25
Day 20..26
Day 21..27
Day 22..28
Day 23..29
Day 24..30
Day 25..31
Day 26..32
Day 27..33
Day 28..34
Day 29..35
Day 30..36

Conclusion..37
Note Pages...............................Begins on 39

Preface

The popular phrase, "*I don't give a shit,*" can have multiple meanings depending on the context of the situation and conversation; but what does it truly mean to *not give a shit?* This 30 day mindfulness program will guide you into the exquisite state of not giving a shit; so that you can live your best life possible, unhindered by the worries, concerns, and problems of other people.

For the purpose of this book, let's define *not giving a shit* as: a state of being in which you are entirely free from the worries, constraints, problems, pressures, and emotions of others, while living happily and content in the present moment. In order to not give a shit, you must break your dependency on the conditioned belief that you must give a shit. Feel free to define *not giving a shit* any way you wish, as long as you recognize it as a release from an adverse attachment to pleasing others or putting others' happiness above your own.

Don't confuse *not giving a shit* with cruelty, apathetic demeanor, aggression, irresponsibility, vindictiveness, insensitivity, or callousness. People often use the phrase, "*I don't give a shit,*" as a means of retaliation, to make a fruitless point, or in an attempt to appear bold or courageous. Truly *not giving a shit* implies that you are free from the constraints of people's problems and worries, so that you can be happy, content, and free to love everyone without emotional obstruction.

When you truly don't give a shit, you can be in a room of various explosive emotions – fights, arguments, conflict, etc. – and be the only person who is aware and present enough to let it all be, without having the desire to contain or put out the fires. When you don't give a shit, you allow the universe to simply be - accepting all of its order and chaos without trying to change it. This mindfulness program will take you through various exercises that'll help you drop your attachment to *giving a shit*; and as you'll see, it starts with your thought patterns and attachments.

The following pages involve a 30 day mindfulness program made up of lessons and exercises to help you overcome patterns of thinking, feelings, and attachments that have kept you in a state of giving a shit. Though these lessons and exercises can be applied to any unhealthy reliance, this program will focus specifically on the experience of giving too much of a shit.

For some readers, they'll overcome the old reliance quickly and will drop the unhealthy thoughts and dependency in no time; and for others, they'll overcome the attachment slowly and gradually. In either case, if you stick with the program, you'll start to witness yourself not giving a shit. Please don't judge your progress in the program, as this isn't a competition and there isn't a goal you must attain. Let the old thoughts, feelings, habits, and attachment simply drop as you work through the exercises and lessons.

It's not necessary to complete the program's days in order, nor should you be religious about completing them successfully. There is no such thing as a successful completion of this program. The bottom line is to observe and awaken, and that cannot be obtained through success, force, pressure, struggle, or competition. Simply relax, follow the program, and you'll begin to not give a shit.

You'll also notice that mindfulness, silence, and stillness are a regular discipline for each day in the program. Because you've been influenced by a dependency based society that demands instant gratification, silence and stillness may seem nearly impossible for you to practice. For this reason, we'll incorporate this discipline from the outset. A quiet and still mind is an incredibly powerful resource, but one that requires daily maintenance. It should also be noted that you're not required to fight the feelings that accompany *giving a shit* during the program; however, if you've already dropped the attachment, then do not pick it up again. The point being: by practicing the following exercises and lessons in the days to come, you won't even need willpower to not give a shit – it'll just happen.

You'll need about 15-30 minutes per day for the program; but feel free to spend more time if needed. The amount of time doesn't matter, as long as you're in an environment that allows you to concentrate without distraction. Also to be mentioned, the last portion of this book includes note pages that you can use with the exercises. It's encouraged that you write down any thoughts, insights, adaptations, lessons, mantras, etc, on those blank pages. The note pages can also be used to rip out and take with you. Feel free to use them as you wish.

One last thing: If you're like most people, you might be dependent on caffeine, alcohol, or sugar to some extent. If you are, do your best to lessen the consumption of these substances over the next 30 days. It's not necessary that you abstain, but can you cut consumption of these substances in half, or more? It's important that your mind is sober and your body relaxed to make the most of these exercises and lessons.

Let's get started.

Let others know you're practicing mindfulness! Post a picture of the cover and include #30DaysNow. Also, don't forget that each exercise has a unique hashtag for online sharing.

Day 1
(Share this experience using #30DaysBreathing)

Exercise:

Find a place without distraction, and turn off all electronics. Sit with your back straight, kneel, or lie on a hard surface (not bed) and remain in silence for 10 minutes.

During these 10 minutes, take deep and focused breaths and hold them for a few seconds each. Exhale slowly. Listen intently to your breathing. Don't try to change it – simply listen, and feel the air go in and out.

*When you're ready, repeat the mantra: "**Be still. Be silent.**" Repeat this slowly multiple times out loud as well as quietly. You might experience boredom or anxiety, but continue repeating the mantra regardless. Repeat it until you're calm and focused. You can continue the deep breathing during the mantra, or take deep breaths during pauses. Don't rush.*

Each of the 30 days will have this time of silence, focused breathing, and a mantra. Except for this page, the end of each day will remind you of the minutes you are to spend in silence and focused breathing; and will also have a mantra for you to practice. You can repeat the mantras during your times of silence and focused breathing, or following. Remember, there is no right or wrong way to do this.

Adverse thoughts and feelings want to fight; in fact, they're energized by fighting. Instead of fighting the condition of giving a shit, meet it with silence and observation. Let the exercises and lessons in this program guide you.

Day 2
(Share this experience using #30DaysPonder)

Exercise:

Ponder this question: Can you remember a point in your life when you didn't give a shit?

Writing is extremely beneficial to the mind; especially when pondering. Write down your thoughts about this particular question. If your mind drifts, then write whatever thoughts emerge. It's okay if you have nothing to write, but ponder the question regardless.

Were you able to remember a period in your life when you weren't experiencing the need to give a shit? If you're like many people, you may have to return to memories of childhood to determine that period. It's not uncommon for a person to experience this attachment at an early age, and continue experiencing it throughout life. We're taught early on, in school and family, to give a shit when people present problems, emotions, reactions, complaints, insults, sorrows, and other such things that deter happiness; and as a result, the attachment to giving a shit is born.

Recognize that giving a shit is a learned thought pattern and behavior with roots. However, it can be dropped quickly and completely; and you have the capability to drop it. In other words, you are not controlled, identified, or dominated by a conditioned attachment to giving a shit.

*10 minutes of silence and focused breathing. Repeat the mantra: **"Drop. Unlearn. Discover."**

Day 3
(Share this experience using #30DaysLies)

Exercise:

On a sheet of paper (any size) write down all the internal lies that you regularly hear about yourself – i.e. within your mind.

Now, tear the paper into multiple pieces, and throw away.

It's common to have an internal voice (or voices) within your mind, playing a record of lies over and over. We eventually begin to accept these lies and let them impact our growth and happiness. Most people you see on a daily basis have these recurring internal voices; and most people are oblivious to them – sort of like white noise. This isn't a mental illness, but a way in which the mind works. We all experience these internal quiet voices whispering untruths about our being. These lies are nothing to fear, but they need to be observed. Writing them down can help you observe and become aware of their deceptions.

The power of silence, focused breathing, and mantras, which you have been practicing, is to draw out the lies. Let them manifest, and observe them. Common internal lies include: *"You're guilty," "You're a failure," "You're a bad person," "You must obey," "You must be liked and accepted," "You don't deserve to be happy,"* and so on. These thoughts are not part of you; however, the deception is to make you believe they are. When you give a shit, many of these lies are planted clandestinely.

*10 minutes of silence and focused breathing. Repeat the mantra: *"**Thoughts are only thoughts - nothing more.**"*

(Share this experience using #30DaysBreathing)

Day 4
(Share this experience using #30DaysHandcuffs)

Exercise:

Put your wrists together. Press them tight together as if they're locked by handcuffs. Actually imagine handcuffs around your wrists.

Now, separate your wrists as if the handcuffs were released or broken – you can do this quickly or slowly.

Guilt implies that you were judged by an authority and were found to be at fault for a crime or misdeed. However, even those who are placed in actual handcuffs are innocent until proven guilty in a court of law. So why do most people accept guilt from others, who are not in a position of authority? Understand; no one makes you feel guilty, even when they accuse you of not giving a shit– it's entirely you shackling yourself. Anyone who attempts to make you feel guilty has guilt of their own to deal with; don't accept it. When you give a shit, you're at risk of be being shackled.

Feeling guilty is the same as placing yourself in imaginary handcuffs and assigning yourself to an emotional prison cell. Don't do that any longer. Many people are taught to assign and accept guilt based on absolutely nothing; most of this deception is learned from childhood, when parents and those in assumed authority threaten punishment and scold. Don't confuse guilt with shame. Unless you committed an actual crime, there is no reason to accept guilt. Drop the illusion. Break free from your illusory handcuffs, and stop giving a shit.

*10 minutes of silence and focused breathing. Repeat the mantra: **"I am not bound by guilt. I am free."**

Day 5
(Share this experience using #30DaysCompliment)

Exercise:

Compliment a total stranger today. You can compliment a cashier, service provider over the phone, server, barista, person at the gym or grocery store, someone on the bus or train, or whomever. It's best if you are not attracted to the person in any way. Compliment someone that you normally wouldn't compliment.

For many people, kindness doesn't come easy. We are taught to judge and avoid from a very early age. You may be a kind person with a good heart; but you're fooling yourself if you believe you treat everyone the same. Spend a few moments today complimenting people you normally wouldn't - not because you dislike them, but because they escape your radar for whatever reason.

As mentioned in the preface, not giving a shit has nothing to do with being cruel, disrespectful, or spiteful. When you truly don't give a shit, you are free to be at peace with everyone, including those who dislike, ignore, reject, and hurt you. Not giving a shit is an incredible act of kindness, because you're always responding in the present moment unhindered by stresses, emotions, and pressures. When you don't give a shit, life is beautiful, because you are not weighed down by frivolous attachments.

It feels good to compliment people, especially when they're overlooked, excluded, and not normally on your radar. Kindness is a self healer.

*10 minutes of silence and focused breathing. Repeat the mantra: **"Kindness heals."**

Day 6
(Share this experience using #30DaysGoals)

Exercise:

On a piece of paper (any size) write down the goals that you've been striving to achieve – i.e. the goals that you believe will bring you fulfillment. For example: a new job, a house in a nice neighborhood, traveling the world, a business, a family, new friends, a degree or certification, building a network, reaching a net worth of a million dollars, etc.

Now, tear up the paper into multiple pieces and throw away.

Goals can be very helpful and useful if they're not obsessed over. However, in the modern world people develop a reliance on goals. Think about all the times you've said something like, *"I need to get that," "I must reach this," "I'll do anything to accomplish that"*, etc. It's often the case that people spend more time worrying about their goals, than freely doing something in the present moment to reach them. Plus, the goal in itself is fleeting, while the journey in the present moment is real and lasting.

The habit of thinking that goals must be met, or else failure ensues, is subtly fixed to dependencies. When you gave a shit in the past, what was the goal? What was it that you felt you needed to achieve by giving a shit?

*10 minutes of silence and focused breathing. Repeat the mantra: **"My happiness does not depend on meeting a goal. I'm happy now."**

Day 7
(Share this experience using #30DaysPassing)

Exercise:

On a piece of paper (any size) write down the name of your current emotion. For example, at this moment you might be feeling agitated, calm, bored, angry, anxious, excited, etc. Whatever emotion you are experiencing, give it a name and put it on paper.

Now, write down "I'm experiencing this emotion in the present moment and it will pass. It's only an emotion."

You can throw the paper away, or hold onto it if you wish.

Similar to how we give certain words credence, we tend to give our emotions a lot of trust. We also tend to blame the outside world for emotions we are feeling: *"They made me angry,"* *"I'm depressed because they made me feel guilty,"* or, *"If they treated me better, I would be happy."*

The emotions you feel are in you, not in the outer world. No one can cause you to feel or emote in a particular way; if they're able to, it's only because you let them. A great way to let a harmful emotion pass is to observe it; and a good start is by giving it a name and seeing it as powerless.

It's commonplace to blame others for our pain. Instead of seeing the emotion for what it is and letting it pass, we've been taught to rely on attachments, such as giving a shit, to manage the emotional reaction. Wake up! Emotions are not you; so stop giving a shit.

*10 minutes of silence and focused breathing. Repeat the mantra: **"I am not an emotion. All emotions that I experience will pass."**

Day 8

(Share this experience using #30DaysDoorway)

Exercise:

Stand in front of a doorway, with the door open. Close your eyes, and take a deep breath. With eyes closed and holding your breath, step through the doorway. Once you have stepped through completely, open your eyes and exhale.

Doorways are amazing tools that can be used for practicing mindfulness and observation. How often do you rush through doors without paying attention to the change of environment? We don't often pay attention or appreciate the transition; we simply rush through unaware that our perspective has changed. This isn't a bad thing; in fact, it's great that we don't stall in front of doorways, too afraid to enter the next environment. At the beginning of this exercise you were in a particular place, and then you stepped through a doorway into a completely different setting. You made a transition without worry or concern, and very naturally. The transition to *not giving a shit* is that easy.

When it comes to physical doorways, we rarely stop and worry about the change of environment – we just walk through and accept the new experience. You can apply this same lesson to decisions that have you stressed, anxious, or worried. Step through the decision to be free from giving a shit and accept the changes; but try to step through aware and grateful. There will always be a doorway leading to new experiences. When you drop the illusion of giving a shit, doorways will be present.

*10 minutes of silence and focused breathing. Repeat the mantra: **"I accept change with awareness and gratitude."**

Day 9
(Share this experience using #30DaysIdentity)

Exercise:

On a piece of paper, write down all the labels and adjectives that you and others use to identify you.

For example, do you see yourself as a daughter, son, mother, father, student, teacher, cashier, friend, engineer, accountant, employee, employer, roommate, wife, husband, etc? And what adjectives do you use to label yourself; for example, do you identify yourself as failed, successful, happy, depressed, moral, unethical, lustful, greedy, valuable, worthless, etc? Don't only write down the labels and descriptions you perceive; but also write down what you believe others label you as: do you believe others see you as a complainer, strong motivator, valuable friend, stupid and incompetent employee, extremely smart and talented worker, etc? Take as long as you need, and fill up a sheet of paper with those labels and descriptions.

After you've done that, tear the paper into multiple pieces and throw it away. Those labels and adjectives mean nothing. They're not *you*. You cannot be defined, labeled, described, or controlled by titles. Most people poison their conscience with such learned vocabulary. They really believe these words hold power – they'll even fight, stress out, become ill, and die to make these words part of reality. The state of giving a shit, as well as most unhealthy states of being, teaches you to identify with particular words, which are only thoughts. Unlearn them.

*10 minutes of silence and focused breathing. Repeat the mantra: *"I am not a label, title, or description."*

Day 10
(Share this experience using #30DaysFocus)

Exercise:

Focus on a natural object or scene for 10 minutes, without distraction and in silence.

Focusing on a natural object for an extended period of time is an ancient practice. How often have you stopped to observe something objectively for more than 10 minutes? When was the last time you've quietly watched a sunset, sunrise, tree sway in the wind, bird chirping, clouds passing or expanding, or just a rock? That might sound boring, but this practice is very liberating. If you look at anything long enough, you start to see it from a different perspective. As easy as this exercise sounds, it's not – try it out, and see how long you can observe without thoughts impeding the practice.

Watching a bird feed may be more interesting than watching an immobile rock; but I encourage you to start with an immobile object, such as a stone or piece of wood. During this process thoughts will emerge – observe the thoughts and let them pass. Don't attach a goal or benchmark of success to this exercise; just observe an object. You might start to give a shit while observing; however, just let that thought come and go.

The goal of giving a shit is to hypnotize you with a false narrative; stealing your attention from the present moment. Wake up to what's around you in the present. Don't let *giving a shit* steal present moment awareness from you.

*10 minutes of silence and focused breathing. Repeat the mantra: *"Be focused. Observe. Be present."*

Day 11
(Share this experience using #30DaysBurning)

Exercise:

Imagine this scenario: It is 3:00 AM. You wake up and realize that your home is on fire. Everyone, except you, is out of the house. You realize that you only have a minute or less to get yourself out before everything is destroyed. You must act immediately.

With such a short amount of time, what do you grab to take with you?

Really consider this scenario; because it happens to people every day around the world. People are forced to leave their homes because of fire, flood, violence, and other uncontrollable factors. If this happened to you, what physical things would you grab and take in such a short window of time? Your cell phone, family pictures, computer, passport, specific files, a project, videogame system, or nothing at all? Whatever you take within that moment will be the most meaningful objects to you. What does this tell you about your desires, attachments, concerns, needs, and habits?

Many things we give a shit about are not worth giving a shit about. People give a shit about their cars, clothes, boats, houses, computers, phones, and other possessions. However, all of these things can be taken from us at any time. Don't ever give a shit about material possessions – they never last.

*10 minutes of silence and focused breathing. Repeat the mantra: **"I am not my possessions. I am free from material things."**

Day 12
(Share this experience using #30DaysBreak)

Exercise:

Find an object that you can break: an egg, a drinking glass, a pencil...anything. In a safe place, break the object of your choice, and be especially careful if it's glass or something sharp.

Don't clean up the pieces immediately, observe the mess and let the pieces sit for at least a few minutes.

Did you break the object, or did I break the object by directing you to break it? And if you believe it was only you who broke the object, did the object allow you to break it? This isn't an exercise meant to release frustration or stress. The purpose of this lesson is to show you that you're not 100% responsible for your perceived chaos, mess, loss, failure, or broken pieces.

Destruction happens in the present moment, and that's OK. We spend so much time worrying about the future, goals, relationships, plans, jobs, situations, and other things breaking into pieces. And when that happens, we tend to blame ourselves or others, because that's what we've been taught to do. Allow breaking to happen; and observe the pieces as well as your reaction to the destruction. Life will have shattered pieces of image, reputation, self, ego, and character...so what? Let the breaking occur. Observe the pieces, and smile at them. Broken pieces are not a problem; however, giving a huge shit about them can be.

*10 minutes of silence and focused breathing. Repeat the mantra: "*I cannot harm or break the present moment.*"

Day 13
(Share this experience using #30DaysSmile)

Exercise:

Hold a smile for 5 minutes. You don't need to do this exercise in front of a mirror; but feel free to do so if you wish. You can even do this exercise during the 10 minutes of silence and focused breathing. While holding your smile, take a moment and feel your face; actually touch the smile and the curvature of your lips and cheek bones.

Have you ever behaved a certain way and then saw your mood change immediately? Physical exercise, such as running and weightlifting, does this for many people. Certain forms of yoga have also been used by people to change their moods. The point is: changing your behavior not only impacts other people, but can also impact your perception of yourself.

You'll notice that while you're smiling during this exercise, you may experience certain emotions. You might feel silly, embarrassed, stupid, weird, or whatever. Continue smiling regardless. In fact, if you're still stuck in the attachment to giving a shit, smile while you're in the grips of that state of being – hold the smile as long as you can; set a reminder alarm if needed. As always, observe your thoughts while you're smiling; observe the thoughts as if they're clouds passing by in a bright blue sky.

Smiling causes an authentic reaction in our bodies and minds that is essentially good. The present moment enjoys a nice smile; so don't give a shit, with a great smile.

*10 minutes of silence and focused breathing. Repeat the mantra: *"Happiness is now. I am happy."*

Day 14

(Share this experience using #30DaysMyLabel)

Exercise:

Most food products have a "Nutritious Facts" label that will tell you the percentage of fat, cholesterol, sodium, carbohydrates, protein, and other important nutritious content in the product. Let's make one for your experience.

On a sheet of paper, write down the words: happiness, stress, anxiety, worry, anger, and depression. Feel free to add other words that describe emotions and feelings that you may regularly experience. Now, next to each word write down the percentages that best represent their measure in your life. There is no right or wrong for this exercise; the point is to become keenly aware of what emotions and feelings you are experiencing more often than others. If you write 70% depression, that is not "bad". Simply be honest with the percentages; recognize them.

Which emotions received the highest percentages? Which received the lowest? Remember, you are not your emotions or feelings; however, you do experience emotions and feelings, and some of them will be experienced more than others, especially during and after giving a shit. If you are experiencing adverse emotions more often than positive ones, then don't let that bother you. Whatever emotion you experience in the present moment, observe it and let it pass. For the negative emotions that come regularly, examine them and let them fade. Observation is the key to understanding.

*10 minutes of silence and focused breathing. Repeat the mantra: *"I am not ruled by emotion. I am here and now."*

Day 15

(Share this experience using #30DaysBreakfast)

Exercise:

If you're reading this before breakfast; have a dinner type meal for breakfast. If you're reading this later in the day, have a breakfast meal for dinner. For example, you can have a chicken salad or pasta bowl for breakfast; or eggs and toast for dinner. Simply reverse your meal schedule for today. If it's too late to do this exercise – switch it with tomorrow's exercise.

Routines can be beneficial for practicing disciplines; however, becoming attached to a routine can cause an unhealthy reliance. When people break from their regular routines they'll often experience stress and anxiety; which reveals an attachment to a strong dependency. It's important to break routine and be uncomfortable at times. The point of this exercise is to change something that you might consider sacred, unchangeable, essential, important, and necessary…meal time. Step out of your regular routine and see that you are not enslaved to it.

When you give a shit, you're actually in a routine of worry, people pleasing, seeking approval or acceptance, building your ego, etc. Within an instant, you can cut out the routine and start living a life free from giving a shit. You might feel awkward when you stop giving a shit, but that's only because there's a dramatic, yet positive, change of being. Accept your new and fresh freedom.

*10 minutes of silence and focused breathing. Repeat the mantra: **"My life is not a routine. I accept change."**

Day 16
(Share this experience using #30DaysCoffin)

Exercise:

Lay down on the floor (not on a bed or couch), with your back straight and your arms at your side. Close your eyes.

Now, imagine yourself in a coffin or under the ground. If this depresses you, do it regardless. With your eyes closed, imagine not being able to open them ever again; also imagine not being able to move your body or speaking ever again. Stay in this position for 10 minutes, or as long as you can.

If this seems gothic or dark, that's only your learned perception of the death experience. There's an ancient teaching that says the way to enlightenment is through a keen awareness of death. The person who is daily reminded that the body will die, and faces this fact head on with a clear mind and acceptance, has nothing to lose and is truly free to live in the present moment. The question isn't whether or not your body will die (because it surely will); the more important question is will you live before death?

Will you truly live before your body dies? The present moment is the only thing you'll always experience. Instead of fearing a pending death, accept it and be thankful for the present moment; and live in it, without giving a shit!

*15 minutes of silence and focused breathing. Repeat the mantra: **"My body will age and pass, but I will always be present – without giving a shit."**

Day 17
(Share this experience using #30DaysPhone)

Exercise:

Turn off your cell phone, or put it in airplane mode, for at least 1 hour, and observe the thoughts you experience. If you don't have any major responsibilities this day, or if you have all you need and don't require the phone, then turn off your cell phone for 12 hours. This exercise works best if you can go 24 hours without your cell phone activated; but go no less than 1 hour. If there are people who are immediately dependent on you, send them a text saying that you'll be unavailable, and then turn off your phone.

Like never before in history, we live in a modern world with a plethora of distractions. These distractions fight for our attention, because money is behind the scenes. Every business is wondering how they can break your distraction from one thing so that you can be distracted by their thing – whether that thing is a product or service. It's a constant war between everyone. Whoever can hold your attention the longest wins the battle; but whoever can make you dependent and giving a shit, wins the war.

Every business, group, network, and social media platform wants you to give a shit about their product, service, or mission; and they use your phone as a means to make that happen. Turn off your phone and prevent it from becoming an avenue that businesses and people use to influence you into giving a shit.

*15 minutes of silence and focused breathing. Repeat the mantra: "**I am not distracted. I am present, here, and now.**"

Day 18
(Share this experience using #30DaysGSR)

Exercise:

Say the words "Guilt", "Shame", and "Regret" 10 times to yourself out loud. Don't rush. Pause between each repetition. For the pause, you can take a deep breath. Your eyes can remain open or closed. Again, don't rush - say the words slowly and observe any thoughts, feelings, or images that emerge internally.

Now, say these words again 10 times, but with a smile.

What futile credence we give words such as Guilt, Shame and Regret. We use these words on ourselves as well as others; they become regular vocabulary for our internal recurring voices. And in the end, they're mere words that hold no power. What would these words be without a facial expression, tone, inflection, or emphasis?

When you said these three specific words, what thoughts came to mind, what did you feel, and was there a reaction in your body? If there is a reaction, such as shortness of breath or a frown, people tend to interpret it as sadness; but this reaction is a learned behavior. We've been taught to feel and think a certain way with regard to guilt, shame, and regret. The truth is: these words mean nothing.

The state of giving a shit, like most adverse states of being, flourishes on these three words and the learned reactions they produce. But see them for what they are...mere words with no power.

*15 minutes of silence and focused breathing. Repeat the mantra: "***I am not Guilt, Shame, or Regret.***"

Day 19
(Share this experience using #30DaysTrash)

Exercise:

Go out and buy a small trash can. You should be able to find one cheaply. If you don't have the funds for this exercise, you can use an empty box or container; however, a small trash can works better for its symbolism.

Designate this specific trash can your "concerns and worries can" (or use any title you wish) – some people benefit from writing this label directly onto the can.

Now, write down (on scraps of paper or whatever paper you wish to use) any concerns, worries, and adverse thoughts that you may be experiencing today, and throw them into the can. Try to practice this every day: quickly write down worries, concerns, and negative thoughts, and then throw them into the can. It may be beneficial to have a supply of scrap paper near the can for easy access.

This exercise may seem simple, but let's go beyond throwing your written concerns, worries, and thoughts away. Designate a few times during the week for sifting through the can and taking out random worries and concerns from days prior – just reach in and pull some out. Observe them, but don't judge yourself. This is a great exercise to learn your negative thought patterns and the lies that grip your conscience. If you stick with this practice, you may gain a deeper understanding and realization into the dependencies, habits, thought patterns, and feelings that may have you giving a shit.

*15 minutes of silence and focused breathing. Repeat the mantra: **"There is nothing to worry about. All is well."**

Day 20

(Share this experience using #30DaysSymbol)

Exercise:

Choose a physical symbol that will remind you to observe and be aware in the present moment. Try to choose something from nature, or that is made of natural material.

The object you choose can be anything, but it's best if it's something that you can enjoy looking at and touching. For example, many walkers and hikers will find a unique rock small enough to carry in their hands. A stone, necklace, bracelet, seashell, cedar block, coin…anything will do, as long as you enjoy it and you can dedicate it as a tool for remembrance.

When you give a shit, you confuse the mind into forgetting you're part of the natural world. The attachment preys on, manipulates, and influences the imagination. Thus, you're taken out of physical reality. By having a symbol of remembrance, you can reconnect with the present moment. This symbol isn't meant to be an idol, god, or icon. Don't think too deeply into this. The symbol is simply a tool to help you remember where you are in the here and now. As long as you're aware of the present, you'll have no desire to return to the hallucination of giving a shit.

*15 minutes of silence and focused breathing. Repeat the mantra: "***All is well. Here and now, all is well.***"

Day 21
(Share this experience using #30DaysName)

Exercise:

Choose a new first name. You can also use your middle name for this exercise.

Now, whenever you're in public this week, introduce yourself using your new name. For example, if you are ordering food or making reservations, use the new name. Whenever you're in a situation that doesn't require your original first name, use the new first name instead. Do this until you have used the new name at least three times.

If you introduced yourself to a stranger using the new name, you may have felt awkward or guilty – as if you weren't being truthful about your identity. Observe the feelings and thoughts that you experienced using the new name. Were you feeling dishonest? Did you feel absent? Do *you* even still exist without your birth name?

We have become conditioned to attach our beings to the most lifeless things. Names are lifeless; they don't exist in reality. They are sounds that are produced; a combination of letters; however, we engrave them on tombstones as if they preserve the person who inhabits the body. Names are not bad; they are necessary for particular means, such as legal matters and family identity; but don't attach yourself to a name. From time to time, practice using a different name to remind yourself that you are not a label, symbol, or sound. Many people who compulsively give a shit do so because they want to protect their lifeless names.

*15 minutes of silence and focused breathing. Repeat the mantra: **"I am not a name, sound, or symbol."**

Day 22
(Share this experience using #30DaysWater)

Exercise:

Deliberately feel the sensation of water on your skin for at least 5 minutes. You can do this exercise in the shower, while washing your hands, taking a bath, going for a swim, walking in the rain, or simply placing your hand in a sink filled with water. Close your eyes if you like.

How often do you deliberately experience the essence of water? We take it for granted every day. It's a remarkable chemical substance in the universe that is necessary for all life. Without it, we wouldn't exist. This one transparent and fluid substance has immense capacity. A large percentage of your physical body is made of this natural substance. Experience it, free of giving a shit.

Every day we jump in the shower, wash our hands, and drink it – but rarely do we take time to slowly and deliberately appreciate our natural response to water. Giving a shit can never give you the energy, sensation, reality, and present moment that water can give. Water is an example of a positive dependency that doesn't bind you emotionally or spiritually. Water doesn't need you; the state of giving a shit, however, does.

There are many lessons that water can teach: fluidity, flow, evaporation, change, motion, stillness, and life. You can't get any of those lessons through illusions such as giving a shit, or any unnatural dependency for that matter.

*15 minutes of silence and focused breathing. Repeat the mantra: *"I am fluid. I change. I flow."*

Day 23
(Share this experience using #30DaysPinch)

Exercise:

Pinch the skin on the back of your hand or forearm until there is discomfort and slight pain. It's not necessary to pinch hard enough to bruise yourself, just enough to feel a small burn.

Did I cause the pain by asking you to do this exercise? No; you caused this pain to yourself – think about this carefully. You even decided how much pain to give yourself, and when to relieve the pain. You can't blame me or anyone else for the pain you just experienced. You were solely responsible. You were also responsible for letting go.

This is easily understood with regard to physical pain, such as pinching oneself; however, we have a lot of difficulty understanding this lesson as it applies to adverse emotions and feelings. How often have you said, and have heard others say, *"He makes me so angry when..."*, *"I'm depressed because she..."*, or *"I'm so frustrated that they..."* No person ever makes you experience negative feelings. It's always you who are experiencing them; and then placing the blame on others. Essentially, you are emotionally pinching yourself and not letting go. People go their entire lives without releasing the pinch. Instead of letting go, they scream at others, *"Release the pain! Let go! Fix this! Stop this! You're to blame!"* Wake up and see that you are solely responsible for letting go of the pain, and you can do it now. No one is to blame for you giving a shit.

*15 minutes of silence and focused breathing. Repeat the mantra: **"I can release negative feelings, here and now."**

Day 24
(Share this experience using #30DaysBathroom)

Exercise:

This exercise may seem frivolous, but give it a try; because it may be one of the lessons that benefit you most.

For the remainder of the day, whenever you use the bathroom, for any reason, take your time with what you're doing. Don't rush through the process, like you may normally do. Focus on taking your time in the bathroom; do every step of your bathroom experience twice as slow. It may even help to say each step: "I am now sitting up straight on the toilet," "I am now putting soap on my hands," "I am now drying my hands," etc.

Most people hurry up their bathroom experience, not realizing what they're doing – forcing, not standing or sitting straight, not relaxing, not washing their hands properly, not drying their hands slowly. They rush in and out, like they have somewhere important to go. Don't be like that any longer. Take your time in the bathroom; it's not only unhealthy for the body to rush the excretion process, but it's also unhealthy for the mind. A rushed bathroom experience doesn't allow you to live in the present moment. Allow the excretion and cleaning to happen naturally with relaxed and focused attention.

The person who truly doesn't give a shit takes their time, exhibiting wonderful patience. Being still, silent, patient, and not rushing…are all characteristics of someone who doesn't give a shit.

*15 minutes of silence and focused breathing. Repeat the mantra: **"Don't hurry. Stay present. Stay still."**

Day 25
(Share this experience using #30DaysLetter)

Exercise:

Write a letter or email to yourself. There is something about using pen and paper that is very effective when writing letters, but feel free to write an email if you wish. Don't send the letter or email, just write it and save it for a day – you can toss it out or delete it tomorrow.

Write anything that comes to mind: It can be advice you want to give yourself, a story from the past, random thoughts and feelings, frustrations and worries, things you're thankful for, etc. There is no right or wrong – write whatever comes to mind in the moment. Try to write at least two full paragraphs.

What was the theme and voice of your message? Was it a positive or negative tone? Were you advising yourself? Did you make any judgments about yourself? Did you start demanding that you should or should not do something? Was the letter full of gratitude? Was there anger and despair? Read the letter as if you were reading it from a friend – is it a letter that would upset you, or one that you would welcome with excitement and a smile?

Whatever you wrote is essentially being written on the tablet of your mind. This exercise is useful for getting to know the internal voice that we all have in our minds. It's an internal voice that can change for the better with observation, acceptance, and awareness. Be aware of your internal voice in the present moment.

*15 minutes of silence and focused breathing. Repeat the mantra: **"I am not my internal voice. I am aware."**

Day 26
(Share this experience using #30DaysWorstCase)

Exercise:

Think of a major worry that consistently upsets you. On a sheet of paper, write down three worst case scenarios for that dominating concern. For example, if someone is persistently worried about failing a specific job, that individual can write as a worst case scenario, "I will do poorly at the job, and will be fired; leaving me homeless and broke." As mentioned, write down three worst case scenarios for your particular worry.

Now, next to each of those three worst case scenarios write, "I accept this." You can either toss the paper or keep it.

Worry is an illness that goes untreated in most people, especially when giving a shit. Think of worry like a cancer of the spirit; but few people know how to treat it effectively. One of the only ways to eradicate worry isn't to fight, ignore, or run from it; but to face it in the present moment and accept it for the illusion it is. You can never be worried about something happening in the present moment – that's impossible; you can only be worried about the future, which is always illusory.

Writing down your worries and worst case scenarios, if they ever do come true (which they rarely do), is a great way to draw those thoughts out of your mind and into the present moment, allowing you to face, accept, and observe them. Accept the worst case scenarios that worry throws at you; knowing that the odds of them happening are slim. You truly don't give a shit when you accept all things.

*15 minutes of silence and focused breathing. Repeat the mantra: **"Worries are not real. They are only thoughts."**

Day 27
(Share this experience using #30DaysStack)

Exercise:

Using objects that can stack (rocks, books, boxes, containers, pillows, etc), stack them slowly and carefully until they fall.

When the stack collapses, smile and laugh.

The lives of many people are spent stacking things for the goal of success, as defined by society. People stack possessions, knowledge, relationships, degrees, money, jobs, toys, businesses, experiences, etc. They stress, fight, fatigue, compete, become ill, and get anxious and depressed through the process of stacking; yet, few people have found happiness. Society tells us that if our stack is high and mighty, we'll have obtained success. What a deception. What are you stacking when you give a shit; or what do you feel compelled to stack? Are you stacking to avoid giving a shit later on?

Allow the stack to fall. This lesson is not encouraging complacency; but instead teaches that real, authentic, and fulfilling experiences can only happen apart from the stress and worry of stacking. When you stack, you're focused on the future and the perceived importance of the stack; and then you have to maintain that heap of nonsense, which requires a lot of anxiety and pressure. Focus on your experience in the present moment; and if the stack falls, then smile and laugh. When you don't give a shit, you allow the stack to fall.

*15 minutes of silence and focused breathing. Repeat the mantra: **"I allow the stack to fall."**

Day 28
(Share this experience using #30DaysCandle)

Exercise:

Light a candle and observe its flame for 5 minutes. Watch it move and feel its heat. Appreciate its energy.

Now, blow out the flame.

(If you don't have a candle, light a match and blow it out; and if you don't have a candle or match, stare at a dim light for 5 minutes and then turn it off.)

The temperature of a small candle flame (and match flame) is around 1200 Celsius (which is about 2000 Fahrenheit). That's a lot of energy! And within a fraction of a second, it was extinguished as you blew it out; or in the case of the light, turned off its energy source. There wasn't a gradual process with delays and stops. You blew out the highly energized flame, and that was it - from 1200 Celsius to nonexistent in no time; or should I say, in present no time.

We think that our thoughts and feelings have so much energy and power. It's not just the state of giving a shit, but all dependencies survive on this deception of power. The truth is: thoughts and attachments don't have energy like the candle flame, though your mind may have been tricked into believing they do. The candle flame is real and powerful; whereas most thoughts are illusory and fictitious.

As easily and quickly as you extinguished the flame, you can drop the habit of giving a shit.

*15 minutes of silence and focused breathing. Repeat the mantra: ***"Dependency isn't real. It can be extinguished."***

Day 29
(Share this experience using #30DaysLaugh)

Exercise:

Make yourself laugh for 5 minutes. Don't stop laughing. You might feel strange, weird, embarrassed, or stupid...it doesn't matter, just laugh. Try to laugh alone and without the aid of a comedy or joke. If you don't know how to start, just start making the noises that typically accompany your laughter.

What feelings did you experience during this exercise? Many people report feeling embarrassed or goofy, which is great; however, most people also report a feeling of relief and buoyancy when they've completed this exercise.

Similar to holding a smile, laughing for 5 minutes is a fantastic way to come into present awareness. If you think about it, humor is necessary for life. How sad is the person who is unable to laugh at the experiences of life? After all, life is funny, even the dreadful and lousy experiences.

If you ever again experience adverse thoughts and feelings that arise from giving a shit, simply laugh at them. Consider how crazy and frivolous it is to give a shit, and your reactions to it; it really is a funny misperception. The entire situation is comical. If you perceive the attachment for what it truly is - a fictitious, impractical, and frivolous idea – then it can be easily dropped. You must learn to laugh at it. When you're tempted to give a shit, just laugh.

*15 minutes of silence and focused breathing. Repeat the mantra: **"Life is wonderful, funny, and real."**

Day 30

(Share this experience using #30DaysThanks)

Exercise:

Take a piece of paper (one that you can keep) and write down all that you are grateful for – these things don't have to be in any particular order of importance.

Next to each thing you list, write "Thank you."

The person who isn't thankful for all that life gives is typically quite miserable; and attachments thrive on that negativity. The truly grateful person can let go of anything at anytime. A thankful person is always a happy person, so practice gratitude daily.

Have you ever heard anyone say, *"I'm so grateful for giving a shit"*? Nobody is thankful for giving a shit; which is a clear sign that it's an unhealthy misperception. However, a few people have learned to be thankful for the present moment experience.

Not only is it unhealthy, but giving a shit discourages a grateful mind and soul. With only one life to live in the present moment, it's important to always emphasize a grateful heart. Spend time with people who are grateful, and do things that nourish a thankful heart in the present moment. Anything that encourages misery and depression isn't worth giving attention to. Be thankful, always.

*15 minutes of silence and focused breathing. Repeat the mantra: *"I am grateful. I am thankful."*

Conclusion

The exercises and lessons in this program taught and encouraged observation, awareness to your present moment experience, change of perception, and awakening to true happiness, which can only be found here and now. You were shown that your negative thoughts and feelings are not caused by giving a shit, or any unhealthy misperception or attachment, but are solely within you and illusory; which means that you are capable of letting those thoughts and feelings pass.

As mentioned at the beginning, there were no goals or measures of success for this program. If you were hoping to find a reason to give a shit, or immediately stop giving a shit, then you may be spending too much time struggling and thinking about shit. This was not meant to be a struggle or competition, but a release. You don't need to gain freedom; you already have it.

Life is not meant to be spent giving a shit, or living with any type of unhealthy dependency. Wake up to the present moment and enjoy your present experience. If you've made it through the program, you are certainly more awakened than when you started; however, don't give up mindfully practicing observation of thoughts and feelings, stillness, silence, deep and focused breathing, allowing everything to pass, laughing, smiling, and being grateful.

Live wonderfully awakened and aware…with or without giving a shit.

Notes for Day 1

(Use this page to write down thoughts, reminders, ideas, prayers, mantras, revelations, lessons, modifications to the exercise, or experiences. If you'd like to share something, please post using **#30DaysNow** or use the exercise's unique hashtag.)

Notes for Day 2

(Use this page to write down thoughts, reminders, ideas, prayers, mantras, revelations, lessons, modifications to the exercise, or experiences. If you'd like to share something, please post using **#30DaysNow** or use the exercise's unique hashtag.)

Notes for Day 3

(Use this page to write down thoughts, reminders, ideas, prayers, mantras, revelations, lessons, modifications to the exercise, or experiences. If you'd like to share something, please post using **#30DaysNow** or use the exercise's unique hashtag.)

Notes for Day 4

(Use this page to write down thoughts, reminders, ideas, prayers, mantras, revelations, lessons, modifications to the exercise, or experiences. If you'd like to share something, please post using **#30DaysNow** or use the exercise's unique hashtag.)

Notes for Day 5

(Use this page to write down thoughts, reminders, ideas, prayers, mantras, revelations, lessons, modifications to the exercise, or experiences. If you'd like to share something, please post using **#30DaysNow** or use the exercise's unique hashtag.)

Notes for Day 6

(Use this page to write down thoughts, reminders, ideas, prayers, mantras, revelations, lessons, modifications to the exercise, or experiences. If you'd like to share something, please post using **#30DaysNow** or use the exercise's unique hashtag.)

Notes for Day 7

(Use this page to write down thoughts, reminders, ideas, prayers, mantras, revelations, lessons, modifications to the exercise, or experiences. If you'd like to share something, please post using **#30DaysNow** or use the exercise's unique hashtag.)

Notes for Day 8

(Use this page to write down thoughts, reminders, ideas, prayers, mantras, revelations, lessons, modifications to the exercise, or experiences. If you'd like to share something, please post using **#30DaysNow** or use the exercise's unique hashtag.)

Notes for Day 9

(Use this page to write down thoughts, reminders, ideas, prayers, mantras, revelations, lessons, modifications to the exercise, or experiences. If you'd like to share something, please post using **#30DaysNow** or use the exercise's unique hashtag.)

Notes for Day 10

(Use this page to write down thoughts, reminders, ideas, prayers, mantras, revelations, lessons, modifications to the exercise, or experiences. If you'd like to share something, please post using **#30DaysNow** or use the exercise's unique hashtag.)

Notes for Day 11

(Use this page to write down thoughts, reminders, ideas, prayers, mantras, revelations, lessons, modifications to the exercise, or experiences. If you'd like to share something, please post using **#30DaysNow** or use the exercise's unique hashtag.)

Notes for Day 12

(Use this page to write down thoughts, reminders, ideas, prayers, mantras, revelations, lessons, modifications to the exercise, or experiences. If you'd like to share something, please post using **#30DaysNow** or use the exercise's unique hashtag.)

Notes for Day 13

(Use this page to write down thoughts, reminders, ideas, prayers, mantras, revelations, lessons, modifications to the exercise, or experiences. If you'd like to share something, please post using **#30DaysNow** or use the exercise's unique hashtag.)

Notes for Day 14
(Use this page to write down thoughts, reminders, ideas, prayers, mantras, revelations, lessons, modifications to the exercise, or experiences. If you'd like to share something, please post using **#30DaysNow** or use the exercise's unique hashtag.)

Notes for Day 15

(Use this page to write down thoughts, reminders, ideas, prayers, mantras, revelations, lessons, modifications to the exercise, or experiences. If you'd like to share something, please post using **#30DaysNow** or use the exercise's unique hashtag.)

Notes for Day 16

(Use this page to write down thoughts, reminders, ideas, prayers, mantras, revelations, lessons, modifications to the exercise, or experiences. If you'd like to share something, please post using **#30DaysNow** or use the exercise's unique hashtag.)

Notes for Day 17

(Use this page to write down thoughts, reminders, ideas, prayers, mantras, revelations, lessons, modifications to the exercise, or experiences. If you'd like to share something, please post using **#30DaysNow** or use the exercise's unique hashtag.)

Notes for Day 18

(Use this page to write down thoughts, reminders, ideas, prayers, mantras, revelations, lessons, modifications to the exercise, or experiences. If you'd like to share something, please post using **#30DaysNow** or use the exercise's unique hashtag.)

Notes for Day 19
(Use this page to write down thoughts, reminders, ideas, prayers, mantras, revelations, lessons, modifications to the exercise, or experiences. If you'd like to share something, please post using **#30DaysNow** or use the exercise's unique hashtag.)

Notes for Day 20

(Use this page to write down thoughts, reminders, ideas, prayers, mantras, revelations, lessons, modifications to the exercise, or experiences. If you'd like to share something, please post using **#30DaysNow** or use the exercise's unique hashtag.)

Notes for Day 21

(Use this page to write down thoughts, reminders, ideas, prayers, mantras, revelations, lessons, modifications to the exercise, or experiences. If you'd like to share something, please post using **#30DaysNow** or use the exercise's unique hashtag.)

Notes for Day 22

(Use this page to write down thoughts, reminders, ideas, prayers, mantras, revelations, lessons, modifications to the exercise, or experiences. If you'd like to share something, please post using **#30DaysNow** or use the exercise's unique hashtag.)

Notes for Day 23

(Use this page to write down thoughts, reminders, ideas, prayers, mantras, revelations, lessons, modifications to the exercise, or experiences. If you'd like to share something, please post using **#30DaysNow** or use the exercise's unique hashtag.)

Notes for Day 24

(Use this page to write down thoughts, reminders, ideas, prayers, mantras, revelations, lessons, modifications to the exercise, or experiences. If you'd like to share something, please post using **#30DaysNow** or use the exercise's unique hashtag.)

Notes for Day 25

(Use this page to write down thoughts, reminders, ideas, prayers, mantras, revelations, lessons, modifications to the exercise, or experiences. If you'd like to share something, please post using **#30DaysNow** or use the exercise's unique hashtag.)

Notes for Day 26

(Use this page to write down thoughts, reminders, ideas, prayers, mantras, revelations, lessons, modifications to the exercise, or experiences. If you'd like to share online, please post using **#30DaysNow** or use the exercise's unique hashtag.)

Notes for Day 27

(Use this page to write down thoughts, reminders, ideas, prayers, mantras, revelations, lessons, modifications to the exercise, or experiences. If you'd like to share something, please post using **#30DaysNow** or use the exercise's unique hashtag.)

Notes for Day 28

(Use this page to write down thoughts, reminders, ideas, prayers, mantras, revelations, lessons, modifications to the exercise, or experiences. If you'd like to share something, please post using **#30DaysNow** or use the exercise's unique hashtag.)

Notes for Day 29

(Use this page to write down thoughts, reminders, ideas, prayers, mantras, revelations, lessons, modifications to the exercise, or experiences. If you'd like to share something, please post using #30DaysNow or use the exercise's unique hashtag.)

Notes for Day 30

(Use this page to write down thoughts, reminders, ideas, prayers, mantras, revelations, lessons, modifications to the exercise, or experiences. If you'd like to share something, please post using #30DaysNow or use the exercise's unique hashtag.)

To be mindful is to experience life in the present moment…it's the only moment we have.

Don't forget to leave an online review.

Thank you!

Printed in Great Britain
by Amazon